S0-DQV-528

JAPAN
The Art of Living

Postcards

(1)

Photographs by SHIN KIMURA

CHARLES E. TUTTLE COMPANY
Rutland, Vermont & Tokyo, Japan

Cover photo: Over a basket of wildflowers is a colorful turtle-and-crane hanging.

Note: These postcards, slightly larger than usual, require the same postage as a first-class letter.

Published by the Charles E. Tuttle Co., Inc.
of Rutland, Vermont & Tokyo, Japan
with editorial offices at
2-6 Suido 1-chome, Bunkyo-ku, Tokyo 112

ISBN 0-8048-1699-9

First edition, 1990

Second printing, 1991

Printed in Japan

Carpenter and gardener join to enhance nature by displaying it through a window.

From JAPAN The Art of Living, ©*1990 by Charles E. Tuttle Co., Inc.*
Photo by Shin Kimura

This entrance to a traditional Japanese house was built to welcome an exalted teacher or lord.

From JAPAN The Art of Living, ©*1990 by Charles E. Tuttle Co., Inc.*
Photo by Shin Kimura

An elegant Spanish-influenced house includes graceful Japanese touches like the moon-viewing window.

Anemones in a goldfish bowl are the focus of an inviting table set with Ching plates and Imari bowls.

From JAPAN The Art of Living, *©1990 by Charles E. Tuttle Co., Inc.*
Photo by Shin Kimura

Atop the chest, a basket of flowers and a stone Jizo, the god of
children and travelers, welcome visitors.

From JAPAN The Art of Living, ©*1990 by Charles E. Tuttle Co., Inc.*
Photo by Shin Kimura

Bamboo is silhouetted on the shoji behind a Bunraku lectern.

From JAPAN The Art of Living, ©*1990 by Charles E. Tuttle Co., Inc.*
Photo by Shin Kimura

Tatami mats lead to the alcove in a traditional Japanese room.

From JAPAN The Art of Living, ©*1990 by Charles E. Tuttle Co., Inc.*
Photo by Shin Kimura

The blending of Japanese art with Western furniture creates
a pleasing effect.

From JAPAN The Art of Living, ©*1990 by Charles E. Tuttle Co., Inc.*
Photo by Shin Kimura

The step chest provides a focal point for this living room, a mixture of the modern and the traditional.

From JAPAN The Art of Living, ©*1990 by Charles E. Tuttle Co., Inc.*
Photo by Shin Kimura

The table is set for the one-pot winter cuisine that is delicious, simple, and enjoyable for all.

An antique Korean bean chest comes to life as the setting for a
handsome collection of smoking pipes.

From JAPAN The Art of Living, ©*1990 by Charles E. Tuttle Co., Inc.*
Photo by Shin Kimura

Bamboo latticework in a round window creates partition while suggesting space.

From JAPAN The Art of Living, ©*1990 by Charles E. Tuttle Co., Inc.*
Photo by Shin Kimura

This living room is a blend of Japanese and Western tastes.

The magic of shoji transforms the bamboo grove outside into alter-
nating patterns of light and dark.

From JAPAN The Art of Living, ©*1990 by Charles E. Tuttle Co., Inc.*
Photo by Shin Kimura

This copper-lined hibachi serves as a coffee table, useful for holding
magazines, flowers, and drinks.

From JAPAN The Art of Living, ©1990 by Charles E. Tuttle Co., Inc.
Photo by Shin Kimura

The fireplace in a reconstructed farmhouse casts a warm glow.

From JAPAN The Art of Living, *©1990 by Charles E. Tuttle Co., Inc.*
Photo by Shin Kimura

Clean white walls and tatami floors contrast with the earthy features
of the beams and reeds on the ceiling.

From JAPAN The Art of Living, *©1990 by Charles E. Tuttle Co., Inc.*
Photo by Shin Kimura

The early nineteenth-century screen is decorated with fans
in a patchwork style.

From JAPAN The Art of Living, ©*1990 by Charles E. Tuttle Co., Inc.*
Photo by Shin Kimura

The pink flowers blend nicely with the blue and white canisters
and dragonfly tiles.

From JAPAN The Art of Living, ©*1990 by Charles E. Tuttle Co., Inc.*
Photo by Shin Kimura

The ultimate art is nature, here filtered through reed blinds.

From JAPAN The Art of Living, ©*1990 by Charles E. Tuttle Co., Inc.*
Photo by Shin Kimura